Scissor Practice

A Preschool Workbook For Kids To Build Scissor Skills

This book belongs to:

Visit **noodlehugpress.com** for more great designs.

Find us on Instagram

@noodlehugpress

A note to Grown-ups:

Activities such as learning to cut simple lines, shapes and pictures can help your child meet key requirements for early standard curriculum. Developing eye-hand coordination and fine-motor skills will help prepare your child for more advanced skills such as writing later on. The activities in this book are for the beginner. Your child will build developmental abilities with each page, growing more confident in their skills as the workbook progresses. Each practice sheet can be cut out by you and given to your child for them to cut and color, with tips and tricks from Sissy Scissors to help the whole process run smoothly and keep it fun!

Scissor Safety

Scissors Selection

Choose safe, child-friendly scissors with a rounded blunt tip.

Getting ready

If the child is struggling with cutting paper, try cutting yarn or clay first.

A purpose built tool

Reinforce to the child that scissors are only meant for cutting paper or other approved materials from grownups, and always supervise them when they are learning to cut.

A place for everything...

Put scissors away in a designated spot when done cutting.

Learning by example

Children learn from what we model to them. Sit in a comfortable position and begin cutting, keeping your thumb up, and moving the paper as you cut, not the scissors. Show the child how to hold scissors by demonstrating, keeping fingers and body out of the way of the blades. Explain to them that two hands are always needed, one hand for scissors, one for paper.

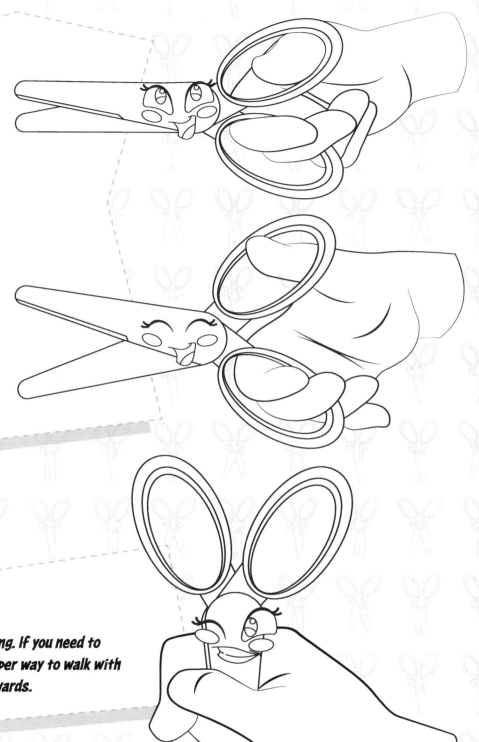

Movement with scissors

It's best to stay seated while cutting. If you need to move spots, show the child the proper way to walk with scissors, holding the blades downwards.

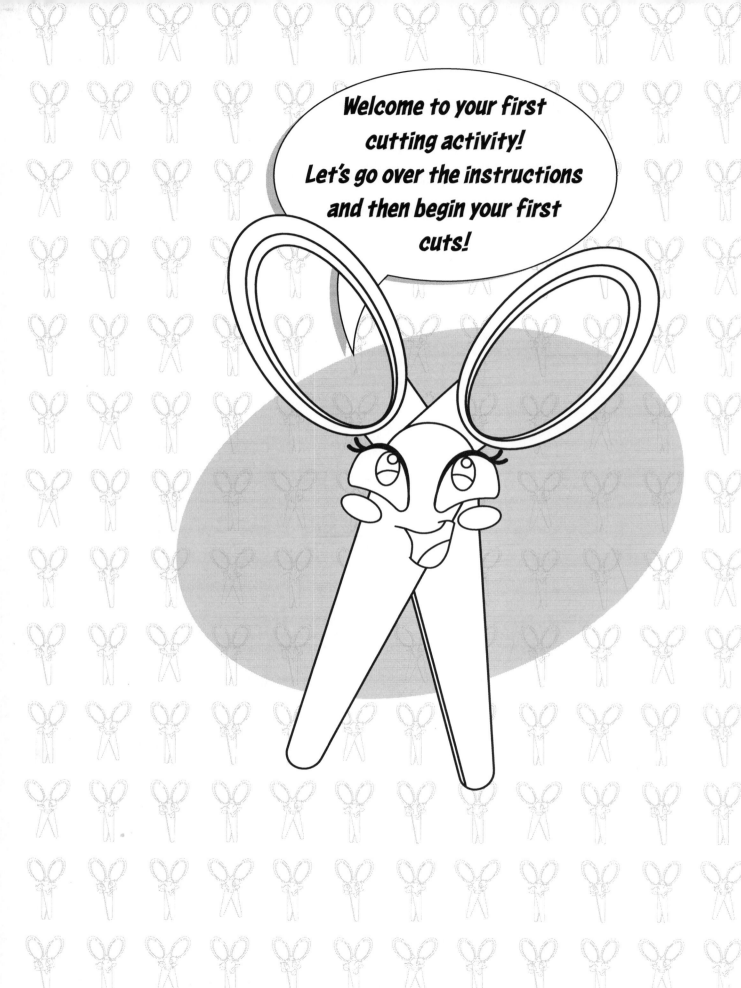

Grown-ups

Cut out these strips along the thick bold outline and give the strip to the child, showing them how to hold the scissors in one hand and the paper strip in the other.

Kids

Cut across the strip in two motions along each line. Snip Away!

Grown-up cut

Kids

Start from the bottom of the page and slowly start to cut towards the top following the direction of the arrows. Remember to keep your thumbnail pointed up!

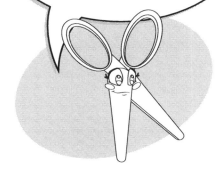

Slow and steady wins the race!

Kids

Start from the right side of the page and slowly start to cut toward the other end following the direction of the arrows.

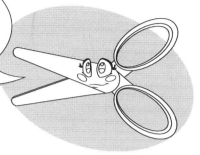

← ← ← ← ← ← ← ←

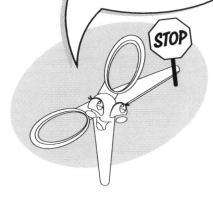

Kids

Time to practice start/stop cutting. Start on the right of the page and make your first cut. Slow down near the end and try to stop the cut at the stop sign. Ready, Set, Go!

Kids

Let's move on to narrow fringes. Start on the right of the page and make your first cut. Slow down near the end and try to stop the cut at the stop sign. Ready, Set, Go!

You're a cut above the rest!

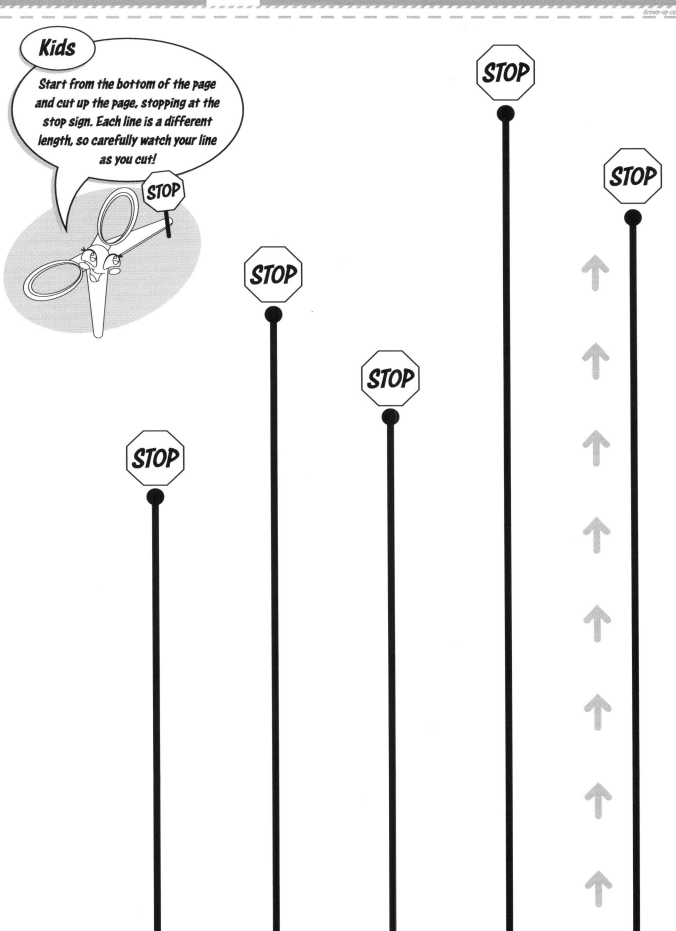

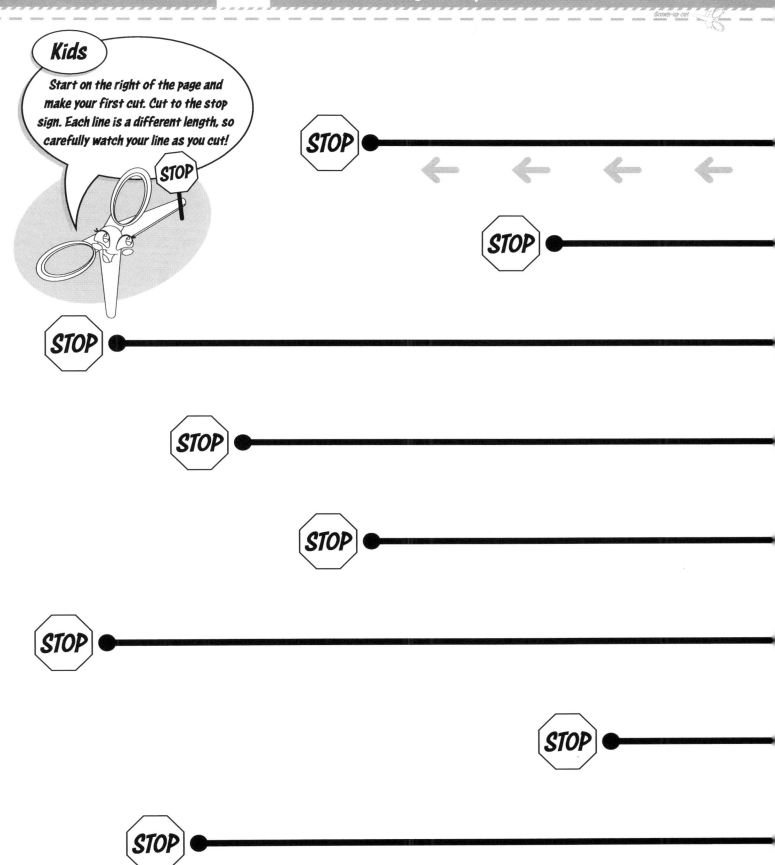

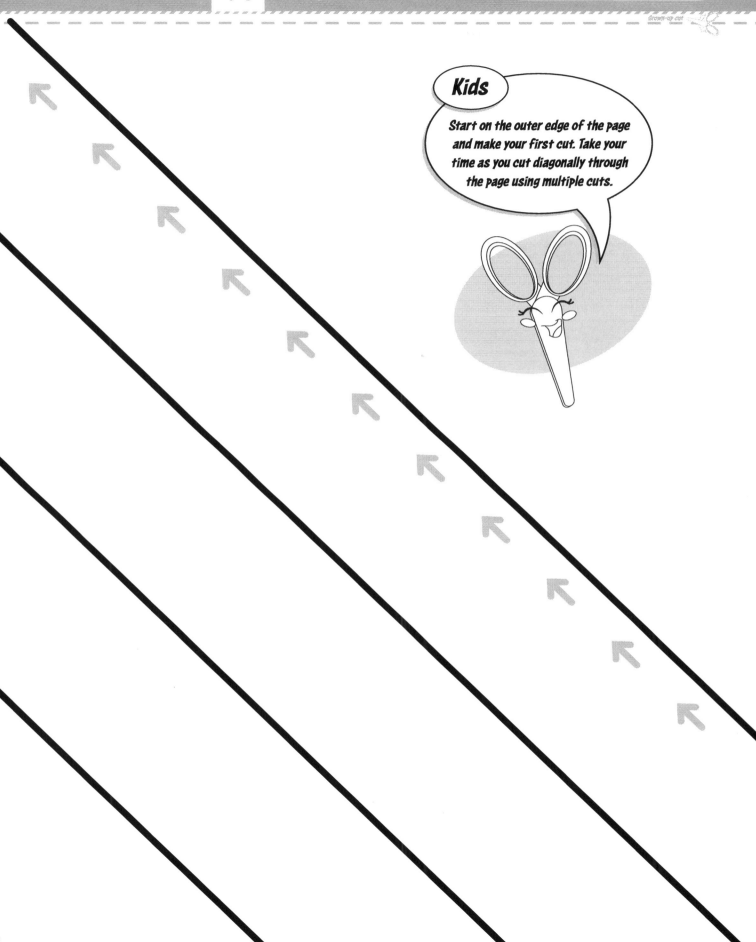

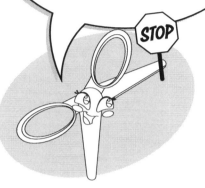

Kids

Start on the outer edge of the page and make your first cut. Cut to the stop sign. Each line is a different length, so carefully watch your line as you cut!

STOP

STOP

Looking sharp! Keep going!

STOP

STOP

STOP

STOP

STOP

Grown-ups
Show your child how to cut these lines by stopping at each angle and changing direction.

Kids
You are doing great! Now onto something new, Angles! Remember, turn your paper as you cut, not the scissors!

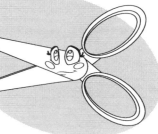

Grown-ups

Show your child how to cut these lines by stopping at each angle and changing direction.

Kids

More angles! Remember, turn your paper as you cut, not the scissors!

Don't worry about imperfect lines. You will get better with time and practice.

Grown-up cut

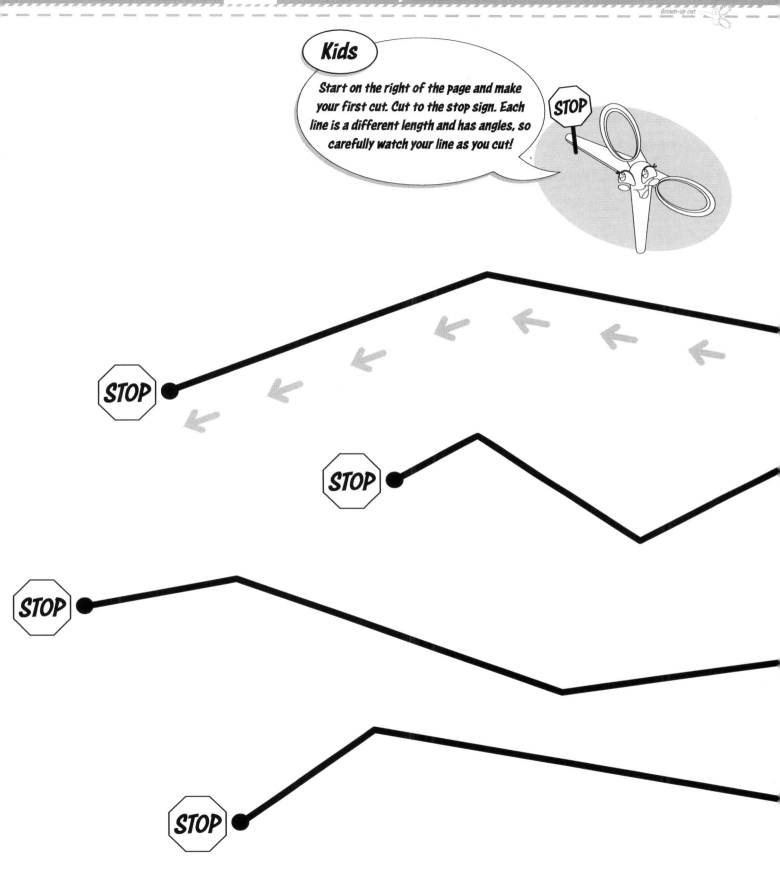

Kids

Start on the right of the page and make your first cut. Cut to the stop sign. Each line is a different length and has angles, so carefully watch your line as you cut!

STOP

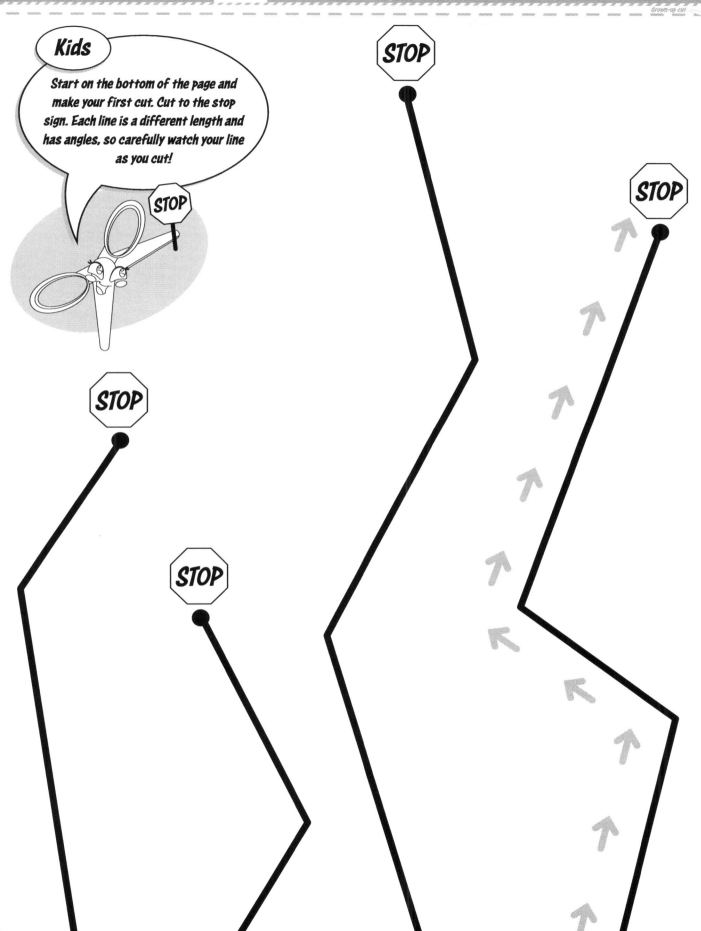

Grown-up cut

Grown-ups

Time to practice curving the scissors with these arcs. Have your child turn the paper as they cut, using multiple cutting motions to follow the arc starting from the bottom of the page.

Kids

Time for arcs! Start your cut at the bottom of the page and work your way up slowly, turning the paper to match the line as you cut.

Grown-ups

More arc practice! Have your child turn the paper as they cut, using multiple cutting motions to follow the arc, starting from the right of the page.

Kids

Below are some more arcs. Start your cut at the right of the page and work your way slowly, turning the paper to match the line as you cut.

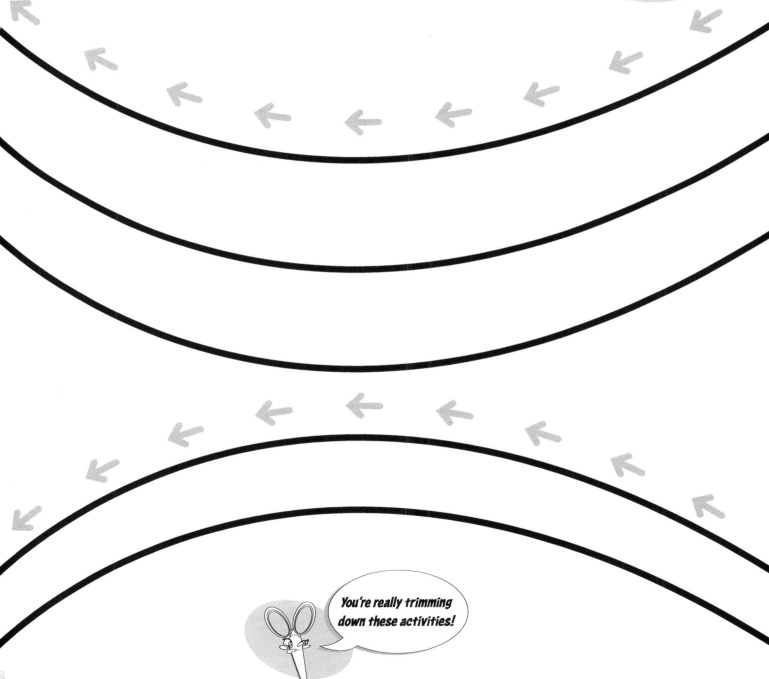

You're really trimming down these activities!

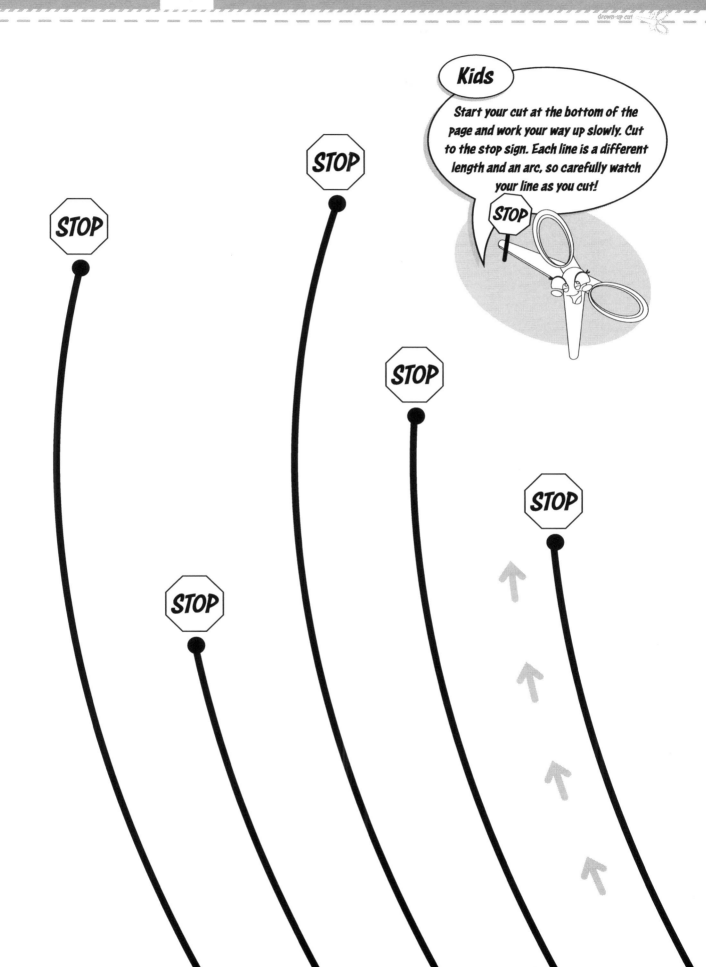

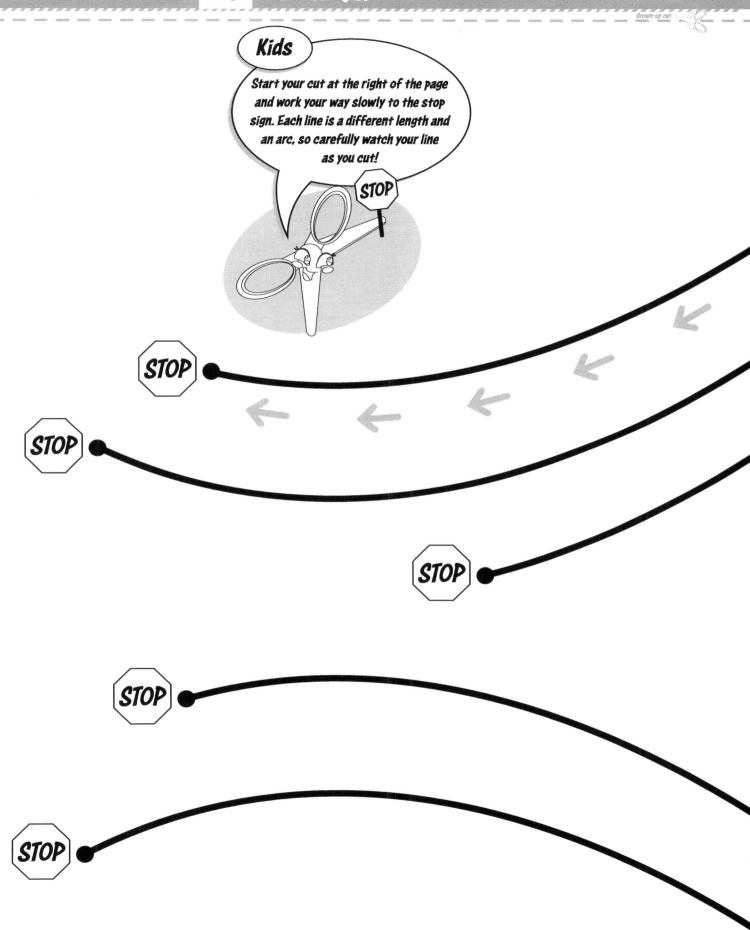

Kids

Zigzags are a more challenging series of angles. Let's practice! Start your cut at the right of the page. Remember, turn your paper as you cut, not the scissors!

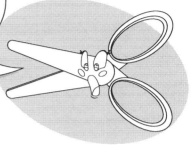

When a problem comes along, you must snip it! Snip it! Snip it good!

Kids

Here are some more examples of Zigzags. Start your cut at the bottom of the page. Remember, turn your paper as you cut, not the scissors!

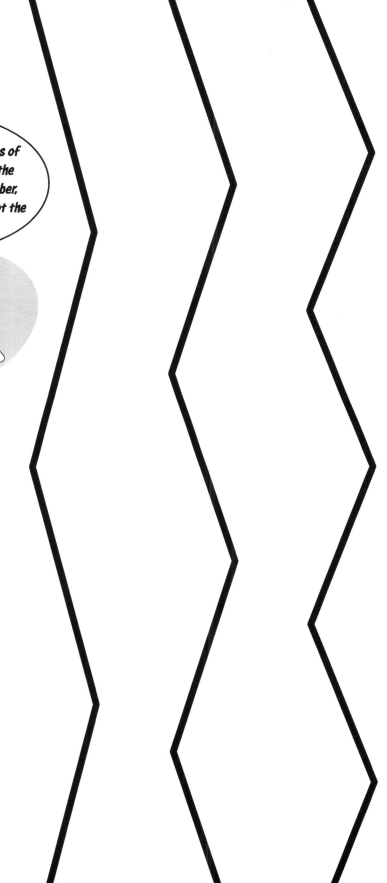

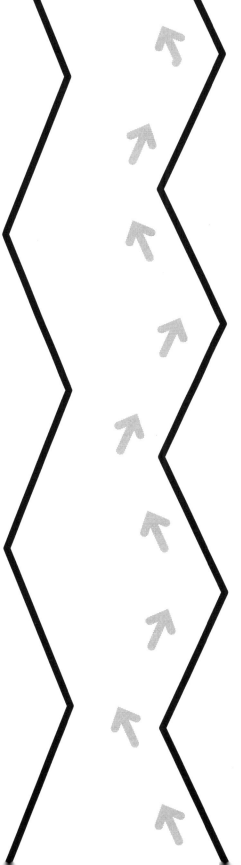

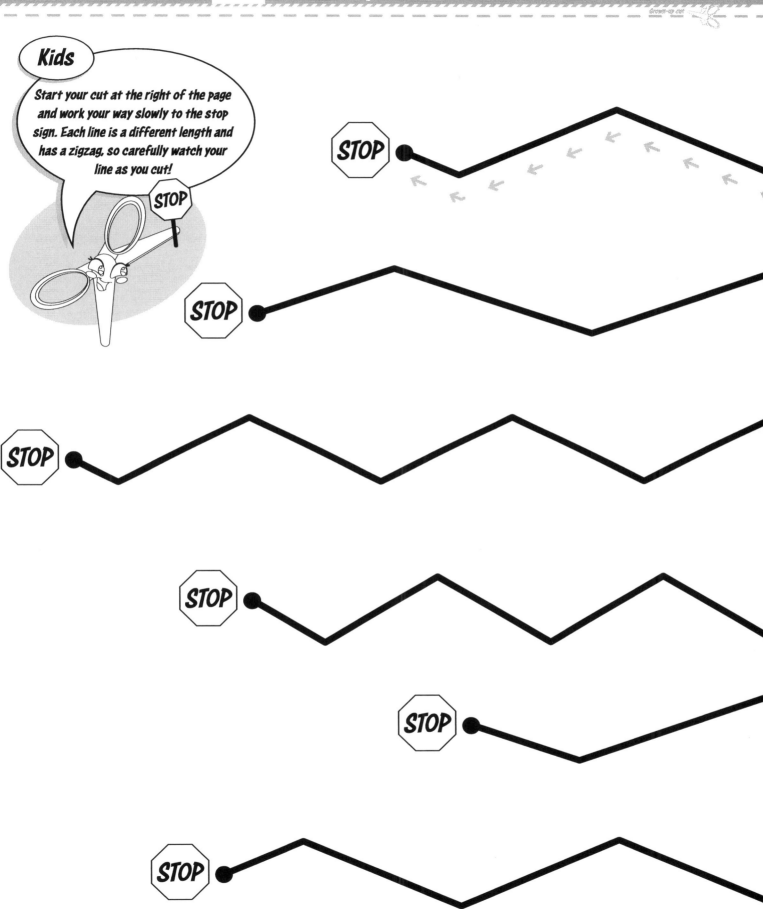

Kids

Start your cut at the right of the page and work your way slowly to the stop sign. Each line is a different length and has a zigzag, so carefully watch your line as you cut!

STOP

STOP

STOP

STOP

STOP

STOP

STOP

Kids

Start your cut from the bottom of the page and work your way slowly to the stop sign. Each line is a different length and has a zigzag, so carefully watch your line as you cut!

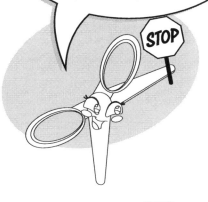

Grown-ups

Have your child turn the paper as they cut, using multiple cutting motions to follow the curves, starting from the right of the page.

Kids

Things are getting wavy! Take your time as you cut and slowly turn the paper to follow the curved lines with your scissors.

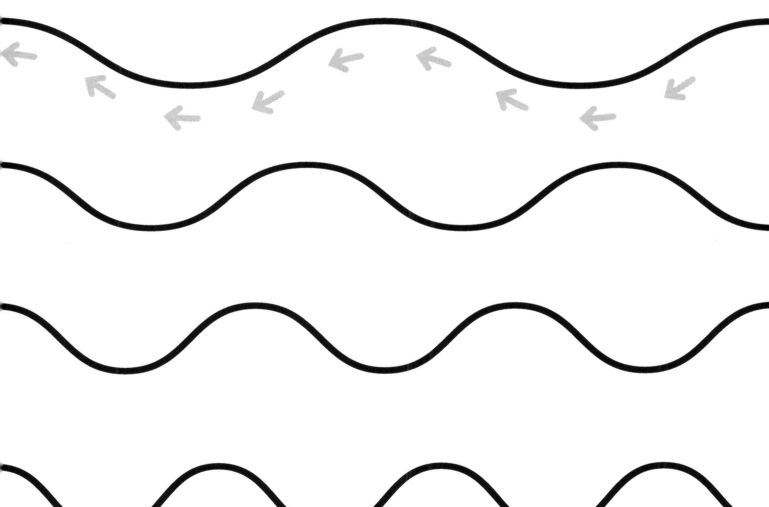

WOW! You're halfway done with this book! Nice work!

Grown-ups

Have your child turn the paper as they cut, using multiple cutting motions to follow the curves starting from the bottom of the page.

Kids

Starting from the bottom of the page and cutting upwards, turn the paper to follow the curved lines with your scissors.

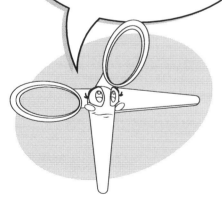

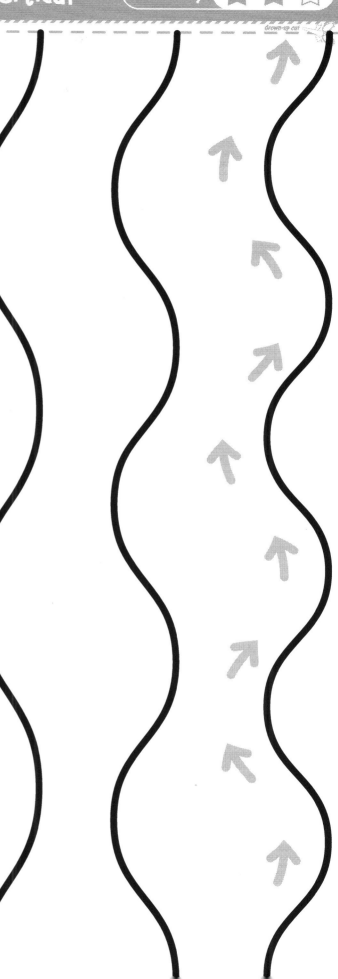

Grown-up cut

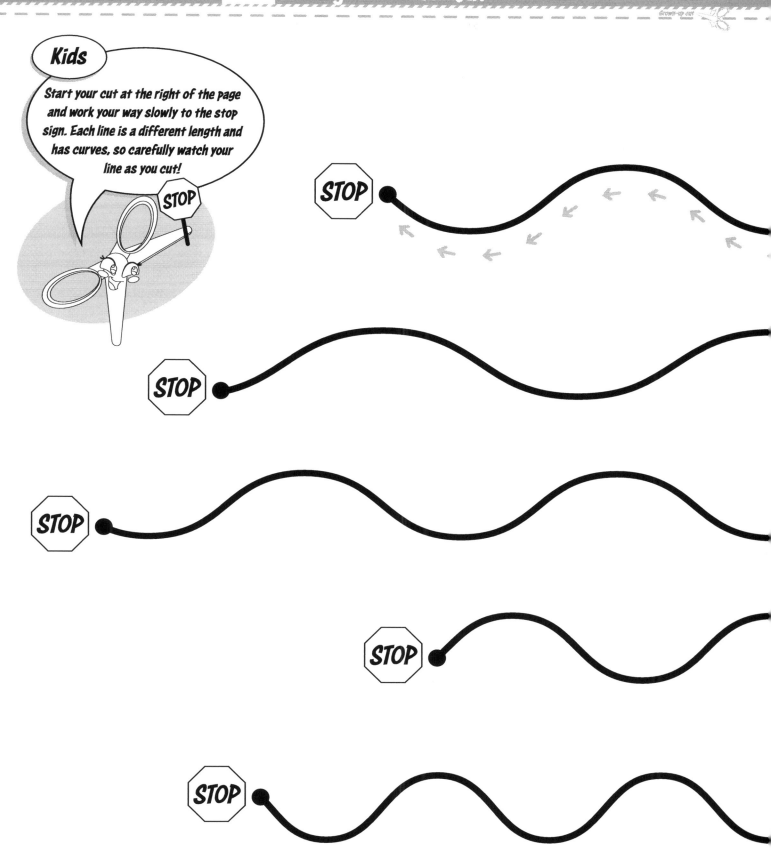

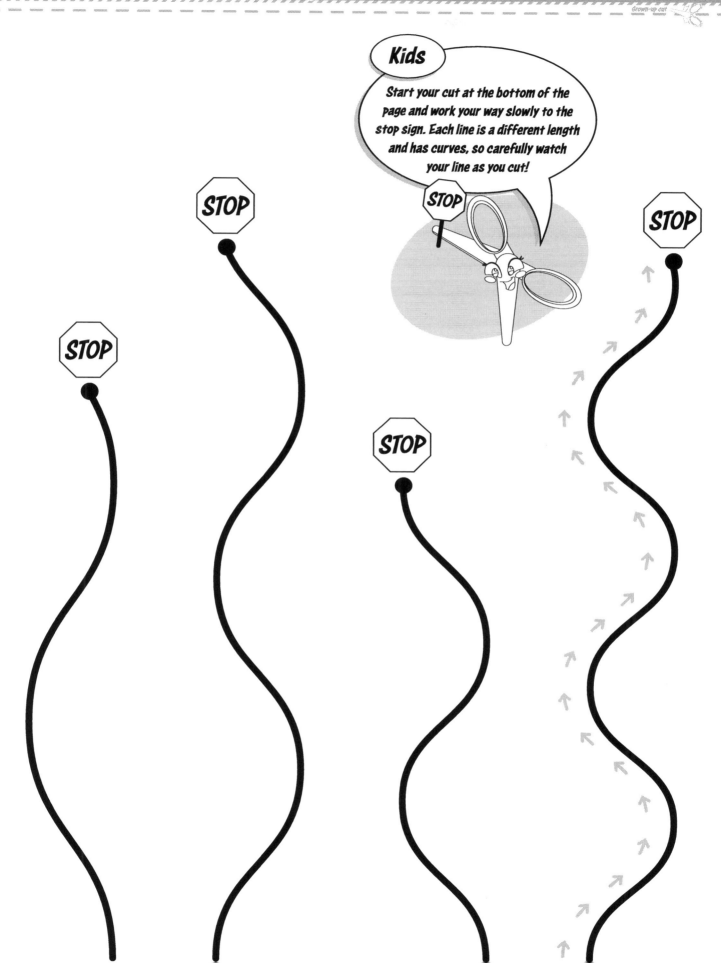

Kids

Remember the three steps for cutting scallops: Turn the page while cutting, stop at the end of each curve of the scallop, and change direction to continue cutting the next scallop! Start at the right of the page.

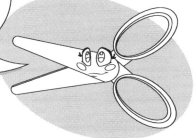

Kids

Remember the three steps for cutting scallops: Turn the page while cutting, stop at the end of each curve of the scallop, and change direction to continue cutting the next scallop! Start at the bottom of the page.

You're a shear genius!

Grown-up cut

Grown-ups

Your child has made it to shapes! On the following shapes pages ask your child what the shapes are and describe the size of each shape. (small, medium, large)

Have them start from the outer corner of the page following the arrows like in the example.

Kids

We've made it to shapes! Let's begin with squares. Start by cutting into one side, slow down when you reach a corner, rotate the page and repeat until the square is cut out.

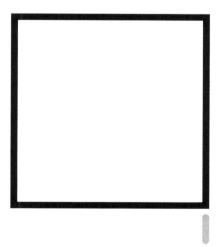

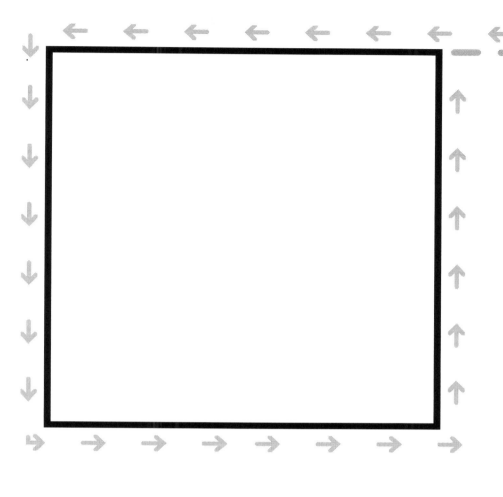

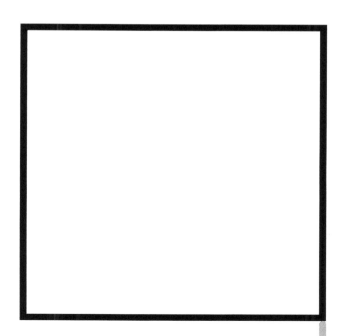

Kids

Cutting out this rectangle is similar to cutting out the square. Start by cutting into one side, slow down when you reach a corner, rotate the page and repeat until the rectangle is cut out.

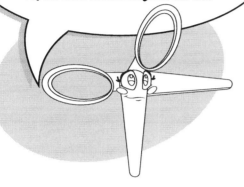

Let's cut these shapes down to size!

Kids

To cut a triangle, remember the technique used on the angles exercise: Start cutting from the line at the edge of the paper, then stop and change direction, turning the paper, not the scissors.

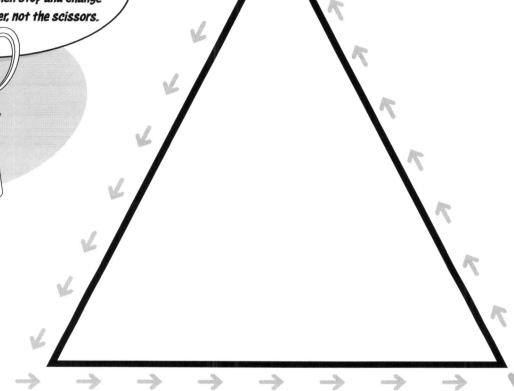

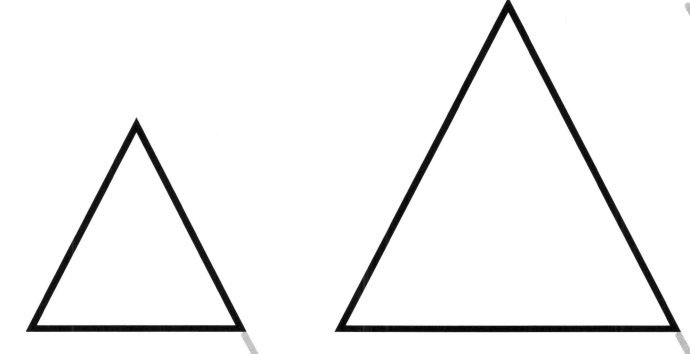

Kids

The earlier exercises for curves have prepared us for circles! Rotate the paper as you follow the curve of the circle.

Let's cut to the chase!

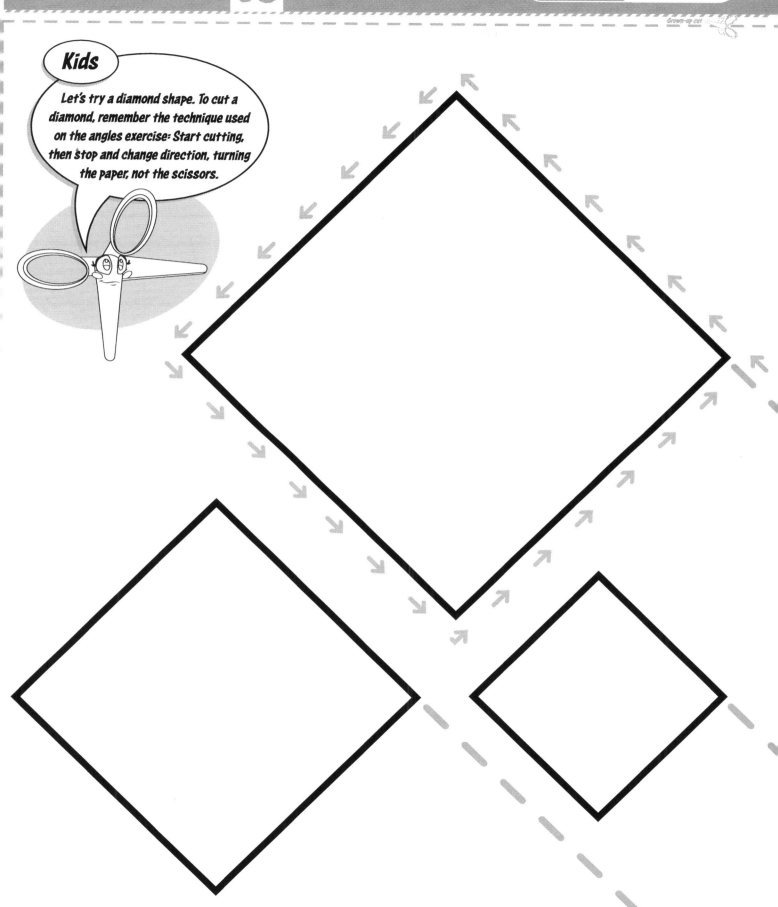

Kids

Let's try a diamond shape. To cut a diamond, remember the technique used on the angles exercise: Start cutting, then stop and change direction, turning the paper, not the scissors.

Kids

This shape reminds me of you, a star! To cut a star, remember the technique used on the angles exercise: Start cutting, then stop and change direction, turning the paper, not the scissors.

Kids

Let's try an oval! Rotate the paper as you follow the curve of the oval. It is very similar to the circle, however the sides of the oval can be taller or shorter than a circle.

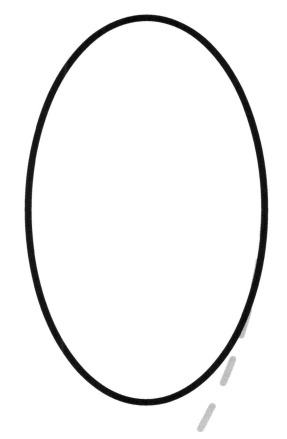
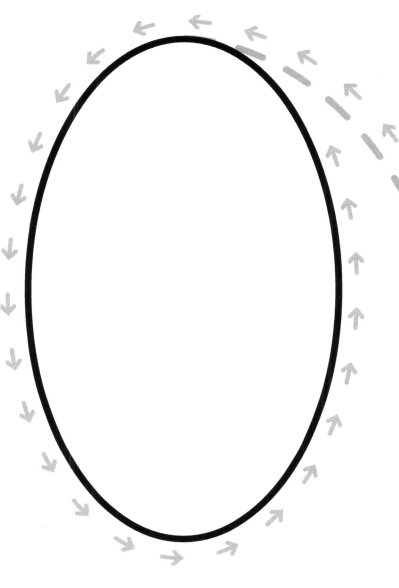
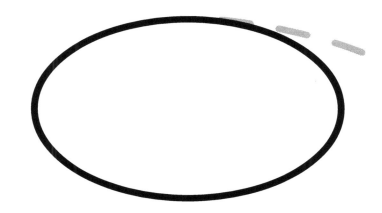

Kids

That's no moon. It's a space station! (The grown-ups will understand). Cutting out the moon is similar to the scallop shape. Turn the page while cutting, stop at the end of each curve of the scallop, and change direction to continue cutting out the moon.

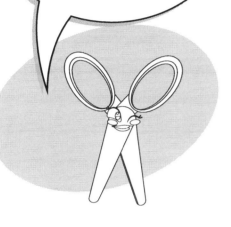
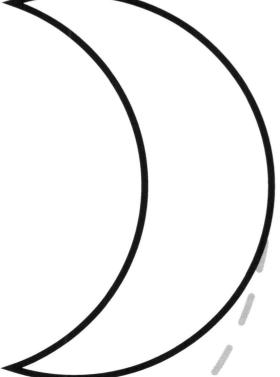
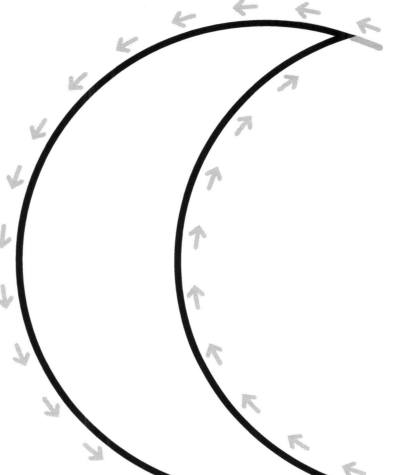

Kids

A lovely shape! Rotate the paper as you follow the curve of the heart. This shape mixes curves, angles and scallops.

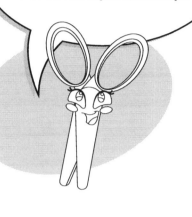

Thanks for trying your best. I am so proud of you!

Kids

Let's try a hexagon! This shape has six sides and six angles. Start cutting, then stop and change direction, turning the paper, not the scissors to match the next side.

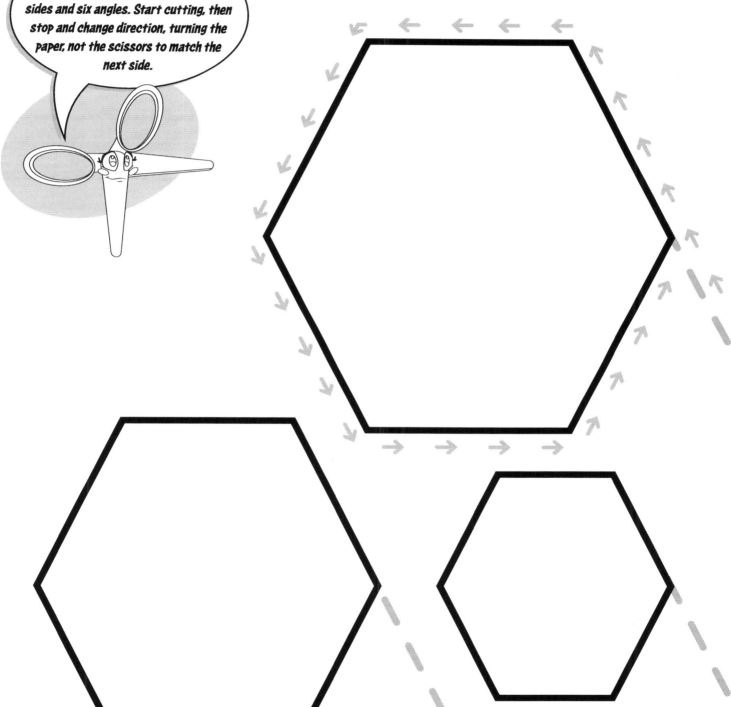

Kids

Let's try an octagon! This shape has eight sides and eight angles. Start cutting, then stop and change direction, turning the paper, not the scissors to match the next side.

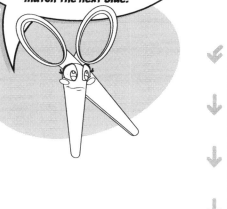

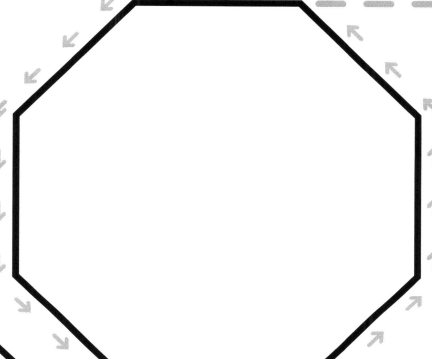

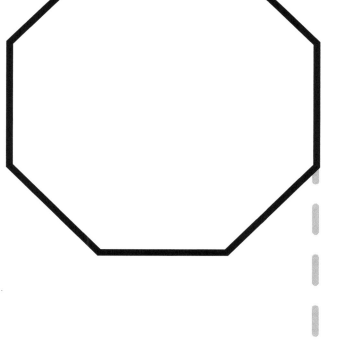

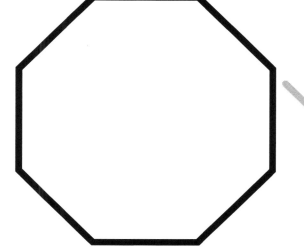

Kids

The most colorful shape! Rotate the paper as you follow the curve of the rainbow. This shape mixes curves, angles and scallops.

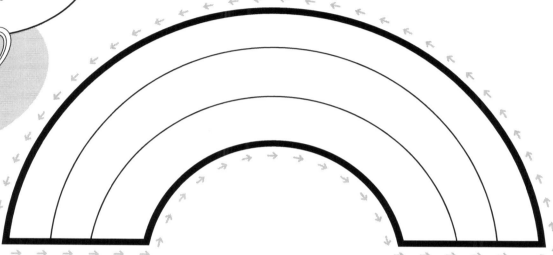

Let's cut for the shear fun of it!

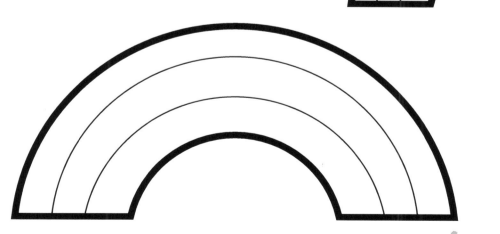

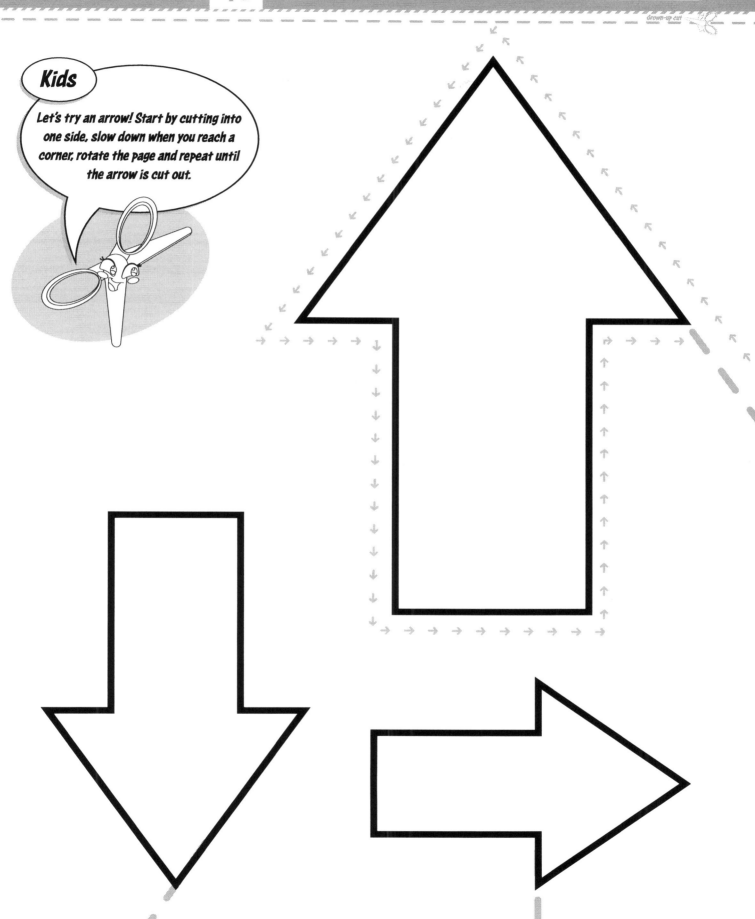

Kids

Let's try an arrow! Start by cutting into one side, slow down when you reach a corner, rotate the page and repeat until the arrow is cut out.

Grown-up cut

Kids

Let's try a house! Start by cutting into one side, slow down when you reach a corner, rotate the page and repeat until the house is cut out.

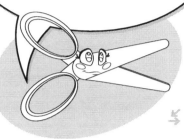

You are doing great! You're almost at the end. Keep going!

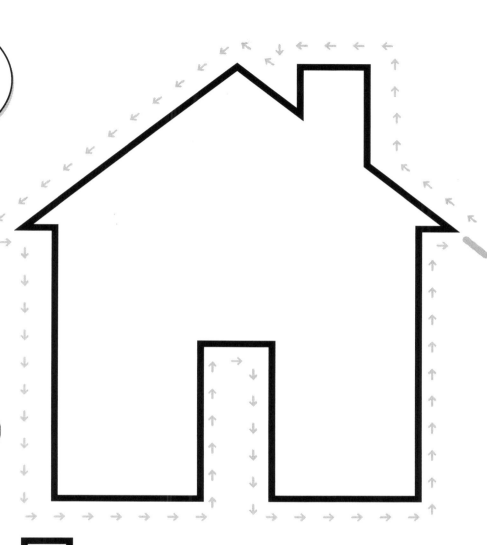

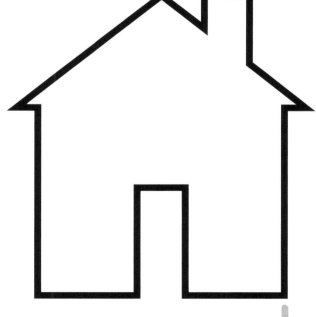

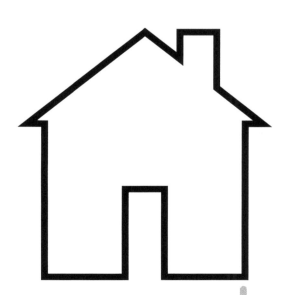

Grown-up cut

Kids

This flower shape has a lot of scallops! Rotate the paper as you follow the curve of the petals.

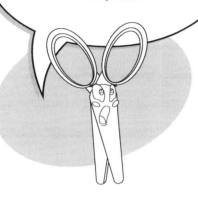

Kids

Balloons are similar to the oval! Rotate the paper as you follow the curve of the balloon, then celebrate once all three balloons are cut out!

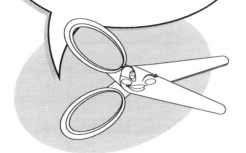

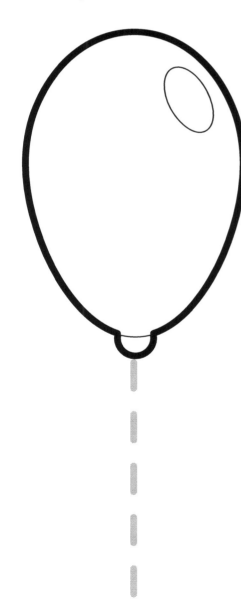

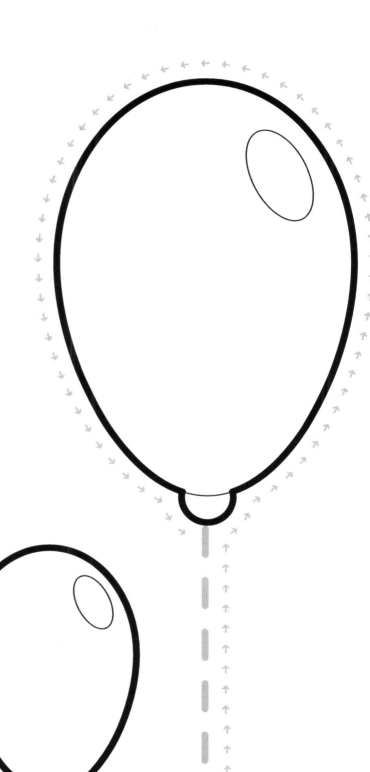

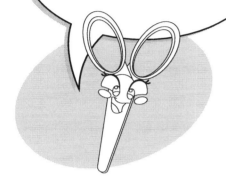

Kids

Drip Drop! Rotate the paper as you follow the curve of these raindrops. This shape mixes curves and scallops.

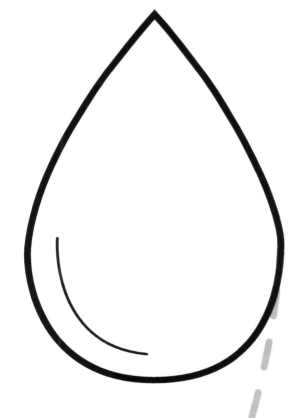

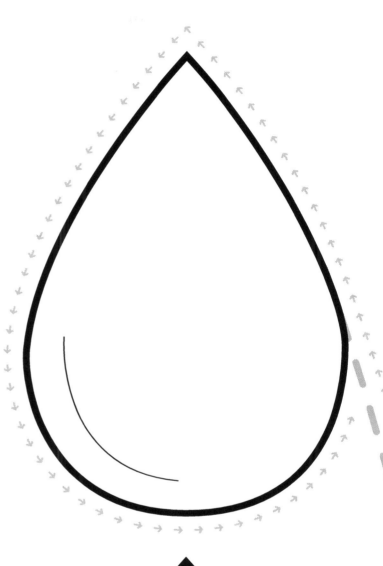

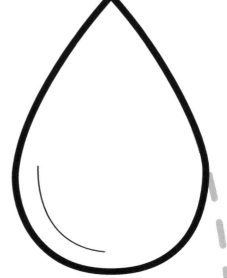

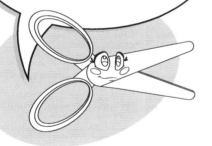

Kids

This cloud shape has a lot of scallops! Rotate the paper as you follow the curves of the fluffy clouds.

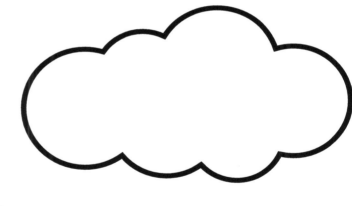

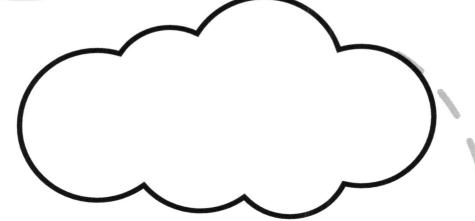

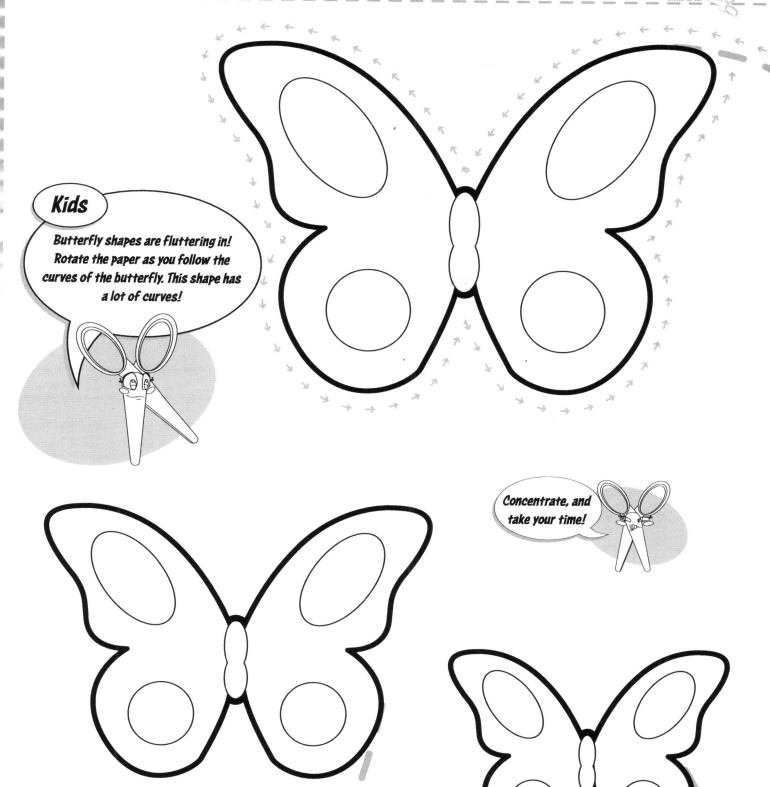

Kids

A sun shape has so many zigzags! Start by cutting into one side and follow your angles, then rotate the page and repeat until a sun is cut out.

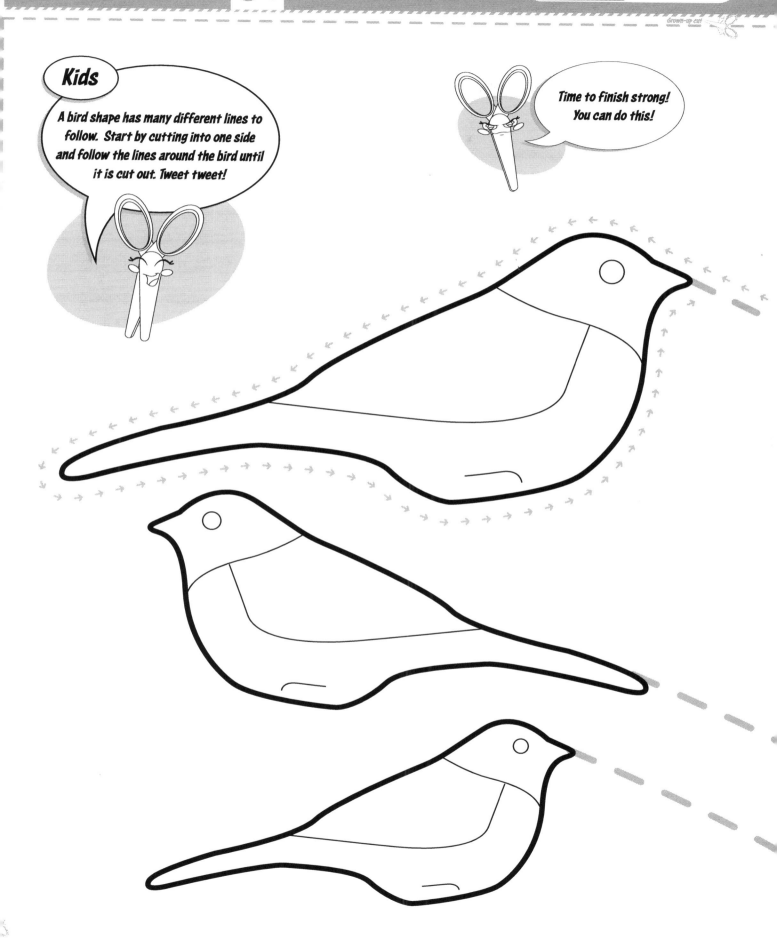

CONGRATULATIONS!

Scissor Superstar!

Presented To:

_____

Date:

_____

Completed

**Beginner
Scissor Practice
Activity Book**

We would love to celebrate your success!
Find us on Instagram **@noodlehugpress** and share a picture
of you with the cut out certificate!
We will happily share your scissor cutting skill with the world!

NOODLEHUG
PRESS

Visit **noodlehugpress.com** for more great designs.

Find us on Instagram

@noodlehugpress

Printed in Great Britain
by Amazon